Seasons

THE TURNING OF LIFE

Seasons

THE TURNING OF LIFE

Moricka & Hannah Burgess

Thanks for your support,

Moricka B

5/09

TATE PUBLISHING & *Enterprises*

Published by Tate Publishing & Enterprises, LLC
127 E. Trade Center Terrace | Mustang, Oklahoma 73064 USA
1.888.361.9473 | www.tatepublishing.com

Tate Publishing is committed to excellence in the publishing industry. The company reflects the philosophy established by the founders, based on Psalm 68:11,
"The Lord gave the word and great was the company of those who published it."

Book design copyright © 2008 by Tate Publishing, LLC. All rights reserved.
Cover design by Kandi Evans
Interior design by Stefanie Rooney

Published in the United States of America

ISBN: 978-1-60604-945-7
1. Poetry: Inspirational/General
3. Poetry: Nature/General
08.07.30

Dedication

This book is dedicated to anyone who has been winded by the bitter cold of winter, felt passion through the heat of summer, blossomed as life brings new beginnings in springtime, or have shed layers of broken promises to be raked away in fall.

Table of Contents

Foreword 11

~ **Spring** ~

Foreword

When reminiscing about my childhood, I had often desired to become a great writer. But my dream was never fulfilled until my girls expressed and pursued their passion to write. Early on in Moricka and Hannah's adolescent years, I noticed they had excellent writing skills. It was always a pleasure reviewing their work, such as essays, poems, plays, and other materials during their school days. Their passion for writing continued outside the school arena even though their lives spiraled in different directions, their love for writing remained the same.

Moricka was often sought out to write mini plays and monologues while attending Adelphi University for campus productions. She also held a position as a freelance writer on social and ethnic issues for Adelphia and Howard University Press. Hannah, unaware of her sister's accomplishments, was paving her own road to glory writing plays and poetry for the community and the Christian realm. One play in particular won her recognition within her state as well as a standing ovation at her national church convocation.

That is why their book, *Seasons,* had to supersede my expectations. In my opinion, their poetry was sensitive, explosive, and detailed—in a most picturesque and distinctive manner. Their writing seemed to speak individually to one's inner being, gripping the soul. It relates to both current events and past experiences, healing old wounds. Let us consider the poem "The Choir of Children." This poem invoked a plethora of feelings: anger, sadness, and hope, while many other poems brought laughter, catapulting readers into a random series of sensations.

Regardless to the massive emotions portrayed in their poetry, Moricka and Hannah seem to have found an approach to writing that can pierce the heart of all mankind. As their mother, I could experience no greater joy than to have lived to see my dream realized through my children. Now I plead with them to continue this journey as accomplished writers.

—*Shirley Burgess*

Spring

The Unattainable Me

It's good that I can't wrap you as a present
Pick you up from under the tree
And call you known

It's good that I can't find you in oceans
Can't misplace you in its streams

Giving meaning to you as emotion
Greet you in my dream

It's good I can't
Play with you, like my children

Meet you as a friend
See you as an enemy

Give you out
As movies lent

It's good, I can't own you

Instead, I'll wake up to you at dawn's light

Enjoying each token every day of every night

For you are unattainable

Happiness

What do you smell like?
At the tip of my tongue

What is the taste of you?
How were you flung?

Who knew you were in man's reach?
Some sought you
Some lost you

Children always smile at you
I wonder do you smile back

People try to package you, in small bundles and
large

I thought I had to take a special trip to find you

Now, after all the living I've lived
My God, you dropped in today

Not All Sunny Days

I crawled yesterday,
marveled at the sky,
wondered about creation,
rested and died.

So you could live.

A Measure of Faith

I see you on the other side
The smiling girl in relentless fight

I see you with your eyes closed
Where no one hears the quiet pictures pros

I see you a second from change

Deeper with your father, seeing his frame

I see you dispelling your secrets

Leaning on Daddy, keeping him near

I hear you breathing the wind
Sucking in destiny

Standing before men

I see you at the brink of day
Too early to worry, too late to stay

I'm watching you, growing in stature
Seeking his face

Knowing his presence
Capturing embrace

I'm watching history shaping

A woman of fortune
Prosperity in the making
Letting out the exhale
Finding his good pleasure
Nothing is your limit
When Abba holds your measure

The Heart of You

I see violets that have never been seen
made of stars incased in your being

I see roses transcending red
flavored by your emotions
gazed from within

I see limelight that dangles in your eyes
in streams of meadows abreast

I see wonders seeded within your soul
beauty acquired shaped by God's hand

I see the unstoppable elements you compose
written in melody, sounds from your soul

I see women in mass
Great and small
Proportionate in sizes
Loved one, loved all

I hear measures that have never been writ:
Different characters in bloom
Giving greatness scent

I see the woman

God, husband and you, the maestro

It's Just Us

In between yesterday and today
there sits heaven

In between the cold of distant tomorrow
and the private piercing of now
here we are

Just left, of fallen love
experienced in the mist of blue weather

In between what I craved
and where you ached—that's us

In between the winter chill of yesterday
and summer's holler, impassioned

In between intertwined bodies
my rested head

A brightened future
and told goodbyes
here we are

In between
the old, the new

a spring sensation, of tasting you
In between—there is you and I

Essence

As...soothing breezes...In warmed apples...And sudden pleasures...by...Brisk Impressions...and...Candle-filled skies...leaves...Sparkling showers...while...Sweetly broken...in...Bathed rivers...stands...Weightless gold...steeped in riches...with human measures...as...Authenticity proven...We're...Marred in clay...Loved...by possession.

The Voices of God

The applauds of oceans
The brilliance of the seven seas

The earthquake's silhouette
and the mountain's silence

A rainbow's tapestry
speeches of thunder

A name of every season
The calm of the Atlantic
The hot beauty of the North and South poles

The flare of the sun
The coloring of the grass
The rainfalls of Africa
The deserts' glory

Horizons conversing
the heavenliest creatures' song

The dancing of the Zulu
the choirs of unmeasured children

A newborn's first breath

Lit

Sometimes we're called
to be a light in the way
in patches of darkness
in dreary days
when light of this candle
is almost out

Sometimes we're called then
to be a light in the way
when morning won't climb
its highest peak
when Saturday is lost in Monday
when happiness smells of grief

Sometimes we're called
to be a light in the way
lit by old poison
that causes no pain
its pertinent ambitions
to leave a mark forever

This mark is you
a light in the way

Expunging the black clouds
lighting the way

A New Dawn

In the newness of the day
I walk the skies
and find each kiss

In ice cream and children's laughter
taste the sweetness of a fresh day
and melodies of life in bliss

Ring the presence of each moment
enjoying lifelong friends

In streets paved with magic
leads ventures unleashed

Today, I can only fathom
gold, hidden in one day's splendor

Rainbow

You stopped me
with a meadow glow

schemes written in the window of heaven's heart
you took me through my threshing place

gripped me within your embrace
composed in streams
arrested at sight

You stopped me
with your magnificence and cumbersome delight

nothing remains the same
marked with signature—Rainbow

Listen

since birds do speak
and we do listen
what is the nature of their tones?

and caught away in oaks of pine
to what hymnals do they fly?

with floats of blue
oft cared colors
the brim of hope they reach

entwined in each symphonic note
in earthen-laced sounds
since birds do speak

Springtime

When winds only cease
in springtime songs
with budded leaves and nature pined

In new beginnings and midnight's stretch

Peaks out
buzzes of lilacs' essence
rose peddles in sweetened breaths

Fragrances of hope flood in the great blue skies
with candy promises bedded in our eyes

As freedom glides in secret winds
promises of promises as spring extends
with blushing songs as spring takes us in

Healing Love

A glimmer of hope
where panes are dried
where daylight's kisses still abide

Where quiet moments are never stolen
and midnight passions
pave book-filled roles

There is a bone no longer split
with destiny's victory joined hip to hip

And the eldest of moments
can never fade
in brick starved passages of children's games

No tattered limbs
where jumps don't hide

As breathes of running
has found new strides

Yes magical memories of love's new name

Sends gifts of fortune
that millions enslaved

In madness of joys

Forever, eternally braced

A Taste of Heaven

A taste of hot apples
And melancholy

A bowl of lavender
With pinkish suit

Song unplaced
Yet whispered ahead

A little girl arrayed
With rainbow smiles

A kiss in the morning
With pigtails delight

An insider course of laughter
After yard play of white

And lilacs and red yarn
Did spin me to bed

As fragrance of tomorrow
Swirls peace above my head

Eternity Travels

Climb every mountain
Jump over every shore
Cascade across the continent
With a word and a phrase
Penetrate every lie
Speak truth to darkness
Impregnate a world
Of every language translate
Burn out
Each bad experience
Pursue the lost cause
Give light to the suicidal,
Envisioning the next generation
Offer the stars
To be their goal
Transcending the possibilities
Making miracles our home

The Way Life Should Be

A child's play on the playground swing...she runs...she jumps...she rolls...when the day is done...the sun has set...she lies down quietly in her room...mother reads a nighttime story... while sitting...on the edge of her bed...she looks up adoringly...with great anticipation...to hear the story's end.

She sleeps...she dreams...of gumdrops...and lollipop fields...where other little ones...often go...to play and grow...when she awakes...she is alone...and she finds her reality...could not be... wished away.

In-Play

Paper dolls
And lollipops
Licorice in batches of strawberry

Musical melodies
On hopscotch parks
Windmills gliding

Rays of songs
Songs of banter
Parades my mid-day

In armed fully rested
Protected in love
Calling beckoned
In glass dolls bedding

Tease Sally and Jimmy
In dirt stained patter

And tomorrow
Iced in daddy's promises

New songs
In park time born

Special Gifts

Wisdom satisfied
In talkative ears
Knowledge finds me
In hidden doors
Crystal reflection
Bounces overhead
In one night's
Decoration
Exasperating balance
Offered one prize
Special gifts
From a childlike bed

Ignite

Put us together and we are lit
Our minds
Our talents
Our gifts

Put us together and we make change
Our classrooms
Our community
Our nation
Our world

Put us together and we do the impossible

We'll create ideas
We'll destroy prejudices
We'll become one
Unity
Strength
Annihilate hate
Call peace
Quicken prosperity
Kill poverty
Educate, relive
Ignite the earth

Summer

Soul Mate

If you reached inside and
pulled out my soul

You would find it covered
with your reflection

Filled to capacity
With your uttered words

Proportionate
To your design

For you are inside of me

Love Note

I thought of that night
And decided to write
But the ink melted
Before it hit the page

Remember that night
That really hot night
When we were alone
And the candles were blown

Remember that hour
Those hours instead
Then we said what we said
The day that we wed

Remember that song
That sweet little tune
That played in that quaint vintage room
Over and over till noon
The night we honeymooned

As we did what we do
You know how we do
Please, please come home soon
P.s. I love you

The Perfect Day

If I could wake up in the morning
Have a toasted cinnamon raisin bagel
With a lot of cream cheese
Daydreaming of you

Noontime
Have a chicken soft taco
With extra sour cream and a mint chocolate chip malt
Then steal away to find you

In the evening
Have grilled salmon with asparagus, garlic, and
mushroom medley,
While drinking a tall glass of raspberry lemonade
Then lay under a star-filled sky—knowing all of you…

What a perfect day that would be

The Virgin's Psalm

I took off my veil
You kicked off your shoes
So scared of you
And of all you could do
Things I didn't
That you knew

Unlike your other women
For me this was new

You put me at ease
By being such the tease
Making sure to take it slow
When I squirmed, you refused to let me go

Unlike your other women
For me this was new

You gave me time to adjust
For the two of us
This has always been true love never lust
Because matrimony was always a must

So I found out
What all the fuss was about
No doubt, no doubt
In that very moment with you
I found out

The Kiss

Kiss me...close your eyes...make me believe this is real...what love...can be expressed in a lip lock...kiss me...and let's not consider the consequence of tomorrow...for the Good Book says... tomorrow will take care of itself...but today... just kiss me...

Kiss me...let your lips...press gently against mine...let the passion surge throughout our being...as a tribe of men...embodied in one moment...kiss me...without letting me go...forever...I refuse to imagine...time...except it be filled...with your kiss.

Kiss me...let us find refuge...in a kiss...we'll climb the mountains high...Mt. Everest...is but a breeze...we'll sail the ocean blue...from here to Timbuktu...mile upon mile...endless sea... endless kiss...today...now...hard...or soft...let us continue to kiss.

Don't Delay

I called to my love
"Come here, come here"
I need to feel your touch
Caress me ever so gently
Come here, my love
Kneel beside me
Lay down, my love
Lay down, next to me
I called to my love
But he did not respond
So I whispered his name
Again and again
Until the heat of my breath
Left an echoing mist
That found him resting
In a far away place
My love, my love
Come to me I pray
Come now
Come quickly
I need you
If for but a moment
Steal away at twilight
I'll lay here waiting
Bare skin adorned

Waiting for you
To cloak me in passion
Swathe me with your flesh
Let us become one
My love, don't delay

When Lovers Speak

Whenever we've been apart for days, we communicate so well...

I'd say, "Sweetie, I've missed you so much..."
As you put your coat in the closet
"So how was your trip?"
You lean against the bedroom door
"So how was the weather? Did it rain?"
The corners of your mouth curve to a smirk
"And your family, is everyone still doing well..."
Your eyes remain concentrated on mine
"Your sisters and brothers, did you have fun spending time with them..."
You walk toward me slow and steady
"Did you get a chance to get out at all?"
You slip up next to me pleasingly close
"Did you get a chance to meet with your business partners, after that..."
You take my hand in yours
"So, I see you're still wearing your wedding band..."
You look down at your hand and then back into my eyes
"I hope you didn't miss me too much..."
The touch of our lips is sweetly soft
"Oh baby, I love the way you converse..."
There is always quiet before the storm

Summer

Hot
Hot
Summer day
Too hot outside
So indoors
We'll play

We'll run
We'll roll
We'll laugh
What we'll do today
Will take some time
In all this heat
I'd dare not
operate too fast

So hot inside
With you by my side
We kiss
We touch
We tumble
We toss
We get so lost
That you forget you were
supposed to leave home

The two of us
On this
Hot
Hot
Summer day

Promenade

If I summoned you,
Would your lips
Find my mouth
And do a dance?

Lend Me You

Lend me your voice if I cannot have your touch
If I cannot feel your gentle caress against my skin
Then let the feel of your words stroke my heart

Lend me your mind if I cannot have your lips
If my love for you cannot be expressed in one kiss
Then let my mind be engulfed in its memory

Lend me your soul if I cannot have your body
If I cannot experience the strength of our interlock
Then allow me daily to embrace your soul

Lend me your dreams if I cannot have this reality
If I cannot have this moment
Then let me escape to your tomorrow

And be taken to a secret place nestled
In the crevice of your yesterday

Making Love

When two become one
There is a sound
While heartbeats pound
In unison
In rhythm
In time
Wedded
Embedded
Movement
As an ocean
Stirring
and waving
Swaying
And praying
Simultaneous
The passion
When two become one

To Know You

You know I watched you
When you didn't see me watching

I noticed your eyes,
oh how bright they get when you're excited
and you clasp your hands real tight
To hide your contentment

I noticed how your simple gaze
out the window intensifies
when you think of a new idea
Or you see something strange, yet beautiful

I noticed your smile
When you think no one's watching
I love how wide your mouth curves
One day I tried to count all the teeth in your mouth

And I know you cry when the pain becomes
unbearable
Though I have never seen a tear

You have your soft tone days
When you are reading a book or reciting a poem
to me
And you speak real loud, actually baby...it's yelling,
Especially, if the Redskins are winning

Some days, when you feel you need to be alone
You escape to a "quiet place"
Where even I am not invited
Because your life holds memories—full of unspo-
ken words

I noticed, you undress me with a smile
To let me read your mind
And I know you cry when the pain becomes
unbearable
Though I have never seen a tear

I'm Gonna Find Me a Man

I'm gonna find me a man
Just as fast as I can

Chocolate covered from head to toe
Who's never gonna let me go

Skin so silky and smooth
Making all the right moves

He'll gently lay me down
Turn my frown upside down

He's gonna cook and clean
Spoken words so sweet never mean

Magic tongue will kiss and caress
Put my body to the ultimate test

Holding me ever so tight
Make love to me from morning till night

When I'm in the mood to munch
Then I'll eat him for lunch

He'll satisfy my crave
Then each night I'll be his prey

This man I'm gonna find
I'll keep him close till the end of time

Possibilities

Kiss me first
Undress me later
Read the inscription
Of my heart
Hear the silence
Rumbling in the madness
Connected by design
Polish my personality
Gaining my trust
Waning with possibilities
I won't be rushed
Clock is ticking
Night fall is at its peak
Streaked with laughter
In a second
We've met
Fumbles are unnoticed
Hierarchy at work
Simple suggestion
Convinced
At midnight, I'm possessed
Puzzled by the factor
Warmth is not a disaster
When love is in the air
At one eve

We close
Without adieu
Your mouth
Stands inquiring
Prêt ail
The next rendezvous

I Love You, Yeah I Love You

I loved you before I knew you
The idea of you is what I loved

Like an artist, loves color then in time
his artwork portrays his heart's work
and this masterpiece occupies space...upon a wall

I love you so much it is near flawless
The only thing I have need of to make it complete is you

Like a basketball player loves the "rock"
And from his youth
studies it, holds it, handles it...with confidence

I love you like a finely aged wine
I've been drunk on you for days

I've sniffed then sipped you,
whirled you around in my heart
And you always come out, the perfect year

I love you like sweet loves chocolate
It is pure destiny

Whether dark chocolate, milk chocolate,
Carmel filled, or mocha latte
Your love is continuously sweet to me

Oh yeah, I love you and I do not care who knows it

You and I

The Sistine Chapel has its brilliance
And it exemplifies a love affair
Between time and a brush

Romeo had his Juliet
As they express love forbidden
Except in death

The ocean shows love toward the world
Each moment it comes to shore
To play kiss and go with the earth

And I have you...

Blown Away

The wind blows and
I feel your presence

I inhale your smile
In each breeze

Your laughter caresses
As it blows about me

And we kiss
Till the world twists into a storm

Then like a tornado everything in our path
Is consumed then blown—away

Echoes of the Day

I rolled to the right and there you were
Quietly above my head, quietly above my head

Kisses and squeezes and hugs
Tongues of love

Laughter and touching and hugs
Tongues of love, laughter and touching and hugs
and hugs

Squirming from bed to floor
And floor to bed, squirming from bed to floor
And floor to bed, floor to bed

Blended on my ceiling mix, paints of roses,
paints of roses
Blended on my ceiling mix, paints of roses,
paints of roses
We played, all over again, all over again

Oh, what a morn I heard it speak
As images of merriment, ran through my head
Ran, ran through my head, ran through my
head

Love

Did you feel it?
The glow of light
The burning,
From inside out...erupting

Did you see that?
From afar
Through the distance
Everything imagined
Mystically...appears

The mountains are not impossible to climb

I fly
Up above the
Atmosphere and sky
I am as light
As a feather, weightless
As light without color

Melodies ring in full harmony
Then, a choir within me sings
Yes, I sing
Without lyric
Without rhyme
I am the music
You are the keys

The sky looks as blue
As the bluest eye

Falling raindrops
Rolling down my body
Like tears
Not from one's eyes
But from the sky
I soar...high
I cannot come down
when I am bound
By love

The Power of Love

You penetrate my body
While making love to my soul

Piercing through my heart with every touch
Like the lance of a samurai's sword

I would gladly die
Knowing that the mere feel of your lips

Gently kissing mine
Would be the breath of life, I need

I breathe you in the morning
I long for your touch in the mid day

I imagine you with each sunset
Lead me, I will follow you

Throughout time, without hesitation
The power of love guides me

Fall

Seasons

When last we met, my fate was chosen
You slammed my doors and froze my eyes

You took hope from my season:

I play no longer in sandy paths
In warm springs and happy moments
Where family sings

You stole precious seconds:
I felt no more of love's hot sensual touch
Brushing my soul, uncovering my inside
Heightened pleasures, trembling breath exposed

Finally, you took my memories:
Times falling colors
Light wind breezes, in rake-filled moments

Now, all I have left is no one to play with
Windows cold and locked that lovers won't touch
No leaves to rake
Only you to hate on frozen doors and grave full
states

The Choir of Children

I hear the cry of children
Sound through a choir of tears

They cry on...
They cry on...

While they wait for someone
To take the time to hear

I hear sopranos scream for compassion
The altos chant of the neglect
I hear the bellow of the tenors
Who have been told—their life is of no effect

I hear the baritones, though dimly
Yet their wail is the worst of all
Since their beckon is so low, you will never know
How long they have been left alone

They cry on...
They cry on...

His Story

The old man sat in the rocking chair
He reckoned of his past so clear
It rocked both back and forth

Then he spoke of olden days
Of times he spent beside lonesome graves
It rocked both back and forth

In a still small voice he began to sing
About loosened chains and how freedom rings
It rocked both back and forth

Then once again he spoke of life
Of youthful souls living with regret and strife
It rocked both back and forth

And then I watched the tears that fell
Like streams running into a filling well
It rocked both back and forth

He cried of all his memories
And in his tears I imagined me
We rocked both back and forth

I Die

The hardest part
was letting go

The easiest
was finding a reason
to obey

The Situation

She has been lost so long
That it's extremely difficult to come home
And all her time is wasting

She's been rampaging through life
With no presumption of what is right
And all her time is wasting

She's been brooding while it's day
Clamoring, "The white coats are coming to take
me away!"
And all her time is wasting

She needs to abandon the man she's with
Because, honey, he has three other tricks
And all her time is wasting

Someone reported she left the other day
'Cause her life was in such disarray
And all her time is wasting

Now I've been watching her for years
I've been too disgusted to shed any tears
And all her time is wasting

The children are for whom I cry
Too much confusion they had to survive
And all her time is wasting

She has been lost for so long
It's extremely difficult to come home
And all her time is wasting

...Some things require repeating

All her time is wasting
...all her time
is wasting,
all her time
is wasting...

The Lonely

If a better tomorrow were possible
I would have left you yesterday
Without fear of waking up alone today

Before I Die

Oh Lord!
Oh Lord!
I'm prayin' now
My God
And King of all

My mind is tire'
My heart is long
Now you take charge
While you hear my call

Oh Lord!
Oh Lord!
You come on down
I been waitin'
I know you
Hear my moan

Come down swiftly
'Cause I told my chil'ren
You know, "Mama ain't got long"

Oh Lord!
Oh Lord!
I'm tire' of weepin'
And havin' to handle
These river-filled tears

On my own

My bones is ol'
I done enough movin'
I done spent these last years alone

Oh Lord!
Oh Lord!
You hear me callin'
Come on now
And get me gone

'Cause I'm full grown
I said my good-byes
Now I'm fixin' to come home

The Tree on Mulberry Lane

There is a tree on Mulberry Lane,
whose leaves refuse to grow
Each day it attempts to satisfy,
the assignment it was born to know

Its branches are flaccid and weathered about
no life in it is found
The soil that is meant to nourish its roots,
they are starved from its desiccated ground

The tree which stands tall is looked upon
by people who pass by
They stop, to stare, to mock at it
through the rustling wind you hear its cry

This tree that is planted to bring new life
is a vivid depiction of Mulberry Lane
For if a life cannot find the will to survive
its demise is unquestionably plain

Showers

life is a shower   rain on me

till i am   wet

till i am   drenched

till i am   soaked to the skin

so i can show the world   I lived!

Everything Must Change

No sooner did I notice you; that I met you
I befriended you, then loved you
I knew you, then lost you
I left you, then I died inside

Seasons change...

The Loud Silence

Too Loud!
The echoes in my head
No sleep, no slumber upon this bed

The sounds
Rebound
The strife
Invades my life

Too Loud!
Yester year won't let me dismiss
No peace, I reach to exist

The earth
Since birth
I'm lost
The cost

Too Loud!
I hide, I run
Once the silence has begun

The silence grows
Yes!
Overwhelming
My soul

Can't breathe
Can't speak
When this silence screams

Too much noise
So, I poise
Would someone please put something on!
This silence is too loud to bear

Reminisce

Reminisce with me
Of olden days
When we left the world alone
When we found a space
In this changeless place
And deemed it
All our own

Reminisce in time
Where you and I wed
And our style of life was new
Where you could love me
As I do you
And the whole earth
Thought it good

The Belly of My Soul

The belly of my soul
Rumbles at your touch
It quivers, it quakes till I erupt

It speaks through the silence
Though no one listens
It waits, it longs
It remains an inconsistent song

The belly of my soul seeks comfort
Yet finds remorse
Seeks pity in its discourse

Through its untimely voice
It seeks to rejoice
Though full of rejection

The belly of my soul cries
It thrives
It drives
and strives to continue

It is saddened when it should be glad
Its recklessness makes it mad
Its mood swings, while I sing out loud
Each time I fall in love

Good-bye

I will see you in my mind
In thoughts of yesterday

I will see you in my dreams
The one place the world could not erase

This Is Not a Nursery Rhyme

Jack and Jill
Ran through the hills
Fleeing from their captors

Jack was chained down
Then stripped of his crown
And Jill became their breeder

The Conversation

What are you doing?
Adorning yourself
With juniper scents
And rosemary oils for him

Are these symbolic, expressions?
Actions,
No reactions
Void of reason

Overwhelmed by love
Endless love
Eternal love
Hopelessly, in love

Tomorrow's reality
We will soon agree
The possibilities you foresee
Can never be reciprocated

Darkness

Sometimes...
the coldness of this world
makes life seem so dark
I do not believe the sun
will ever show its glow

Today...
the darkness that invades my mind
is so inconceivably black
that I will not recognize the light
once it chooses to appear

Revelation

The sun shines so bright in the day
With every touch of its rays
The world begins to glow
As it reveals things
Once hidden

When night falls
The light of the moon
Descends quietly upon the earth
Escaping and uncovering
Even the most dismal places

As day and night continue to mock life
By revealing truth

Dark Secrets

There are secrets in the dark
As the wind whistles at the world

There are hands beneath the covers
While the moon begins to shine

There are kisses, strokes, and feels
Though twilight beckons for the dawn

There are secrets in the dark
Each night the dark is dread

Fall

The leaves were green before
The climate was warm

The flowers had not blossomed till now
Life had no form

The seas were settled and still
The winds refused to stir

The palm trees bent from left to right
My life is but a blur

Winter

Winter

You don't fool me
I know who you are

This isn't the first time
You broke these gates

I used to be afraid of you
I hid all the time

You came blowing through here
Knocking down my mind

Anger, savage things
Fill your cruel head

Promised dreams
Only to take them instead

Frozen branches
I can't think of my next mood

You ripped down my presents
With your beastly bark

You sent cold clatter
In place of a warmed heart

Out of 365 days
I only have to survive you in one phase

I know the stench of your bite

I know who you are and fate holds your night

Gold Digger

All my life, pearls played me
I took control
Made diamonds dig for me
Like my mindful bone
He gave me diamonds for dirt

His one hundred thousand, yearly pocket

No more fake leather
Why rabbit,
Instead of fur
His hours worked
Makes loving plain
For bedded essentials

Wall Street moments
Line clients up—line my wardrobe
My big pocket honey, takes care of business

Lining me with silk
Caressing me—big strong money
Helping me forget
Bad, poor Buick days

Cashing in with love songs
A Porsche and Lexus

All my life, I watched pearls jade me
Sterling silver, tried to be my man
My honey, He knows
My only lover

He's my first—second
After all
A girl can't snuggle up
To millions

His one hundred thousand, yearly pocket

Comes without papers
One day, I'll drape him
Like foolish busted curtains
Until millions—replenish my soul

The Legacy

This legacy of pain
Danced through my house

Gave entrance through my rooftop
Trickled down my heart

Made camp in my backyard
Waiting for every child to grow
Gave ungodly knowledge
Attested to their soul

This legacy of pain
Has decreed a great proclamation
Curse my daughters
Forgot my sons
Making me a fool

This legacy was buried, once in a crypt of love

Unrepentant mothers, sold daughters
Spattered on tables—with false love

Blackness has crept upon us
Every daughter's daughter end

Left with its betrothal
As new owner of this old brittle house

Needy

I tasted the empty kitchen
Licked the floor clean with turpentine
Found soft poison in jelly beans
Touch base with hunger
When no parents were found
Begged for underwear
Left behind Tia's bracelet
Faced off with the school counselor
Till all my truth spilled regret
Each moment in my solemn past
Gave no room for greater nightmare's stories
Till the day I left my broken home
And paid strangers took me in...

Mean Mother

I hated my children
And love them to death
My confession was their cruelty
Their life my only step

I bore them as prizes
Took no reward for their success

I destroyed them in acknowledgements
I corrupted them by bad manners

Inception was my fool
I harbored every bad word

In worrisome greed
I cloned their names
My fame to fortune
Was succeeding them
My only poison—their shame

I took their lives
And renounced my only glory
For the stories I rocked them to sleep

Sold them for fear of old age
And now their only treasure
Is what I believed them to see
The mother of their youth
In yesterday's childlike dreams

With War and Pride

There is a bond
Built on the bricks
Of men
Mortar
Of blood and sweat
Mixed with American pride
Colored with the bullets
Of Indians, Africans,
Hispanics , Jews
All facets of cultures and tribes
Opening their eyes
Outliving desecration
Standing in history
Uncharted assimilation

There is a bond
Crawling in holes
Creeping amongst air raids
Living in the midst
Of feuds

There is a bond
Transcending the nature of man
Transforming multi races
In scripted in the plot
Of an American flag

A nation inbred
By the differences of its neighbor
Held to gather with the fabrics
Diversity and willingness
Entrusted to change

The Heart's Unmentionables

You drop something
Oops, it vanished away
The subconscious can't hear
Sounds like thunder
Runs like a child
Nourishment is its bloodline
Squalls like hummingbirds

But quieted
Injected by the heart
Pants erratic pleas
Silenced, simple seconds

A bloody mess
Dressing for travel
Discrete prowess

Angles of Perception

One family
Two children
A father, a mother
The broom is cracked
The basin is broken

The world has a lightning storm
Walking the corner

At the market down the block
In the school yard
A lightning storm

Until sleet, snow
Wind, rain
Hail, black ice
Take me home
From the portal
From which they came
This is the model family

Be Careful What You Eat!

I saw the belly of my soul
Bulging to tell me its dark truths
Truths of fools and truths of youth

I saw the belly of my soul
Ghostly pampered with nuggets I possessed

Feeding on anger, dismay, and rage
I saw the belly of my soul

Hidden within, the names and times I suffered
Blinded with wrestled unease
In the belly of my soul

No bread, no butter or greasy chicken to digest

I wouldn't feed love's hunger or forgiveness
But I kept regret

I digested every secret from young to old
I saw the belly of my soul and my belly saw me

My diet was built on hate
So cancer replaced my fate

For in my belly and soul
Cancer ran deep

Grandma's Sayin'

Choose your words
My mama said
But Papa wasn't listenin'
Just before bed

Choose your words
Make them positive woes
Papa had a bad day
So he gave us ranting in our heads

Choose your words careful 'cause
"The good Lord hears"

But, Papa wasn't 'fraid of him
As he sifted cruelty in our ears

"You'd betta be watchin' everything you say"

Mama done said, but at the hour when we
Buried Mama

I'd wished Papa yelled instead!

Dead Man Walking

Two of us are walking
Living on one road
Grazing the grass of life
One feeds
The other eats
Till friends realize
She's walking alone
Walked amongst the dead

In a blink
You're contaminated
Sucked happiness dry
Barebacked the children
Smiled in this last cry

All seasons shifted
Alaska befriends us
I shared a road
One road
Amongst the dead

Anorexia

I'm not well
I'm fat
My clothes can fit two of me

I'm not hungry
My stomach just speaks in baritone

I'm not ready
I can't do the run

My flabby foes keep slowing me down

Don't be concerned
I'm fine
Can't you see?

I'm determined to put on my prom dress
Mama and Papa
You've got to know
I'm not your chubby cheeked daughter anymore

Just before bed
The meat
The chicken
The rice
The greens
The pie

The cake
All my enemies fill my head

I won't taste of them
My dress almost fits

Mistakenly, I slipped into my sister's dress instead
She was always so fat—now that she's ten

And still my dress won't fit

Zero (I forgot her name but not her story)

The quantum zero
Gone without useful sense
Heard sounds of zero

Her borders, her homeless banner
No source of life

Gasless sounds, in running engines
A glimpse of zero, intruded today

Perplexities of life
With her wiped words

Solemn sunken weight
Grinned displeasure

Hostile mementos
Hospital birth, pressed death doors
Lungs of distress, dark hopes live

Grandma's pleas of faith
Homeless bound
Direction and redirection
Home found and home without

From 1946 till now

Skin to bone
Mental zone
Schizoid and bipolar

People passing through her words
Never heard, never known

In quantitative sum equals zero
From birth to death

Daddy's Little Girl

Hugs that go quietly
Scars that fill my heart's empty space
The burden of being me
Missing my calling
As your little girl
Chocolate candies
Dainties and spices
Perfumed in niceness
Bargain basement prices
I am Daddy's little girl
Pockets full of bows
Earrings and bracelets
All decorated for dedication
In the hall of fame
As Daddy's little girl
In my mural
All I'm left
Pictures everything you want me to be
Only in the mirror, I saw on yesterday
My reflection only saw me

Without Shame

I saw you in the window
Your image scowled at me

No longer petite
But enormous with improprieties

I blew on the window
It blocked out my face

Ashamed of my misfortune
Tired of the maze

Some ten years later
Remembering the woes

Glimpse of a future
Now faded away

Not ashamed
When I took him
Spent my youth and age
Miserable from the beginning
Too proud—set in my ways

Now the clock is done ticking
School is out

Finally, ashamed of my past reflection
Regretting the days, shame was out

The Clothes of Pain

In every fleeting moment, the clothes fell
With every thought, the clothes fell
In disagreement, the clothes fell
In ritualistic devotion, the clothes fell

Pressures found in little wonders
Unspoken bitter verbs
Defeated dreams
Mazes faded by family and friends, the clothes fell

As days went and came
Disappointments stayed in
Every yes you turned to no, the clothes fell

Sunny Sunday morn
Climbing mountains, lurking piles
In undressed houses, the clothes fell

Waning twisting turns
Devastating awakened realities
All clothes to hangers missed, the clothes fell

Screams of banshees
Gasps of air
Orphaned stares
Clothes fall no more
Clothes to bury in
For clothes are to silence as no voice is to death

Daddy

Who will cry for me?
I can't walk
Who will see me?
Who will call?

Please, someone handle
I know not my name

Yet, five fingers
I see every day

Just before
My mourning cry
I speak the only words
I can pronounce

Yet and still words aren't my friend
For the five fingers, come now and again

Loose me, help me,
See me, discover me
Mother dearest

As I work on my vowels
Though words aren't my friend

Who else can I turn to?

The five fingers, the last thing I saw

A Woman's Issue

I looked in the mirror
And it rejected me

I saw the shadow
It looked like my twin

I saw the frame
And spat at an old friend

Reflection was her name
And she went too far

She told me of bumps
And lumps in solace housed

And spoke of words
I knew nothing about

Lies, lies
As I took off
My blouse

One breast was enlarged, the other was gone
The mirror cracked and the reflection spoke
No more

The River's End

How desperate can one be?
His love I need

How desperate can one be?
His child, his name

The anguish, the pain
Madness and insane

He plays
I'm game
His child
His name

If I could take time,
With my hand the clock rewind

His name, my pain
My anguish, insane
No hope, no help
The clock, it stops

My shoes, lost my feet
One bridge
One ledge

Clock stops, ease dread
I seek, watery bed

And my river called to me
The cold, the ice

Covers my face
I think twice,
"His love, his child"

No time left, I'm river bound

Gutted

I gave, you took
I bought, you stole

You purchased me without price
I lay down and you doctored your right

I left all
I followed you
In bed
In money
Obedient to the form

You turned me upside down
Bared my ribs, sold my butt

Grazed my fat—your wallet thick
Left me bleeding from broken truths

Gutted me without a knife
Marred me inside out
Took me back to childhood
Gutted me out

Put me on the market for new buyers
Sold by the pound